The Great Riddle of Being

A Guided Tour of Jim Holt's "Why Does the World Exist?"

CURIOUS READER

Copyright © 2012 Curious Reader

All rights reserved.

ISBN: 1481278460
ISBN-13: 978-1481278461

CONTENTS

	Preface	i
1	Introduction	1
2	The mystery of being	6
3	The power of nothing	12
4	Finite vs. infinite	20
5	A theological explanation of the world	25
6	Physics and the multiverse	34
7	Mathematics and the real world	42
8	The de-materialization of the world and consciousness	48
9	From goodness to existence	54
10	Possibilities and selectors	59
11	The self and death	64
12	Highlights	71
	Notes from Curious Reader	76

PREFACE

Metaphysics seems to be an unlikely subject for a whodunit story. And yet Jim Holt's recent book "Why does the world exist?" is subtitled "An existential detective story". In it the author travels around the globe, follows many leads and interviews numerous experts in search for an answer to the ultimate crime mystery: what or who brought this universe into being? Solving this riddle requires a good deal of abstract thinking with the help of advanced concepts and theories from philosophy, physics and mathematics. If you are afraid of getting lost in the maze of existential problems and paradoxes, this short guide with its explanatory notes and highlighted main points will make an indispensable companion to the original book.

1 INTRODUCTION

The question "Why is there something rather than nothing?" hardly ever occurs to the proverbial person in the street. Such a question can be seriously considered only by metaphysicians or children. The standard answer to it that a child might hear is that God created the world out of nothing. But this answer leaves us with the question of why God exists. Perhaps, as some suggest, God is so perfect and powerful that he can explain his own existence. (However, some philosophers respond tongue-in-cheek to this argument that God is so perfect that he doesn't even have to exist.) Nevertheless we may still wonder if there is an alternative solution to the riddle of being which could be available to non-believers as well. At first glance, it looks like atheists are in a worse position than believers when it comes to the explanation of the world's existence.

It is imaginable that science could one day discover a mechanism which would be capable of explaining not only how the world is but why it is. However, physicists, among them Stephen Hawking, remain doubtful. The main problem with a scientific explanation of why the world exists is that such an explanation should be presumably given in terms of physical causes. But physical causes are part of the physical universe that stands in need of explaining, so they cannot be used as an explanation. To put it slightly differently, we can trace the origin of the universe to *something*, but this cannot explain why there is *something* rather than *nothing*. It appears that no scientific theory is capable of bridging the gap between non-being and being. In response to this challenge many naturalists simply aver that the existence of the world is a brute fact which does not admit any explanation. The world just is, and that's that. But the main problem with this solution is that it leaves us with unfinished business. Some philosophers insist that all important truths must have a rational explanation, and isn't the truth that the world exists an important one? For instance, the German 17th-century philosopher Gottfried Wilhelm Leibniz introduced the Principle of Sufficient Reason, which states that every significant fact should be explainable by something else.[1] If we deny the possibility of an explanation for the world's existence, doesn't this imply that the fact that there is something rather than nothing is random, irrational, or perhaps even absurd?

So far the above considerations have been implicitly based on the following two assumptions: that reality consists of (at most) two types of substances, the material and mental ones, and that to explain something is to give a causal story involving one or the other type of substance. For instance, the impact of one billiard ball causally explains the other ball's movement, and the panic of investors causally explains a stock market crash. But it may be pointed out that the dualistic ontology of mind and matter is not a fully adequate representation of reality. Some philosophers believe that there is yet another category of objects besides the mental and the physical ones. This is the category of abstract, mathematical entities. It is hard to imagine that mathematical objects, such as infinitely dimensional spaces, could exist in physical space-time or within finite human minds. Some philosophers, Plato included, insist that abstract entities occupy the realm beyond space and time. But the problem is that abstract, unchanging objects cannot figure in usual, causal explanations. This means that we have to look for types of explanation other than the causal type.

Generally speaking, to explain something is to make it more understandable, or intelligible. The Greek philosopher Aristotle distinguished four explanations of the causal type. One of them involves the notion of a final cause, which is an end or a purpose of something.[2] Such "teleological" explanations seem to be rather crude when it comes to natural phenomena, but perhaps they are just right for an explanation of the universe as a whole.

It may be speculated that the existence of the universe could be somehow explained by mathematical objects, or objective values, or maybe logical laws. A non-theistic explanation for the world's existence might be available to us if only we could find the right type of "algebra" – an algebra of being, so to speak.

The theistic explanation of why the universe came into being uses the familiar concept of a personal, all-powerful and all-knowing God. But why should the ultimate creating force be understood in this way? According to the most recent variant of the Big Bang theory, known as chaotic inflation, creating a universe does not require any supernatural powers. It could be even done in a laboratory with the help of technology only slightly more advanced than ours. All that is needed to get such a universe going is a fraction of a gram of matter, and the rest can be achieved by a runaway inflation. All the billions of stars and galaxies can be created from the negative energy of the gravitational field. Because its space would be extremely curved, from the perspective of our universe the newly created one would be incredibly tiny, perhaps even smaller than an elementary particle. But a truly tantalizing possibility is that our universe might have been created in such a way. Perhaps the creator of our universe is just a physicist hacker. The physicist Andrei Linde makes a half-joking suggestion that such a hacker could encode a secret message about him- or herself by manipulating the fundamental physical constants of our universe, so that our physicists would be able to decode and read it. The hypothesis that our universe has been created by a scientist and not a supernatural divine being could explain the apparent imperfections in its design. However, the question of who created the science hacker still looms large.

2 THE MYSTERY OF BEING

Philosophers by profession seem to be particularly well prepared to discuss the question of why the world exists. Unfortunately, a systematic and comprehensive philosophical analysis of the greatest riddle of being has yet to be developed. For now all major schools in philosophy, and even individual philosophers, offer radically different perspectives on this issue, ranging from denying the very intelligibility of the question to providing long-winded but not particularly enlightening answers. In the pre-philosophical and pre-scientific era the question of the origin of the universe was an exclusive domain of myths and religions. But virtually no mythology traces the origins of the world back to nothingness. In many creation myths the universe springs from some type of primeval substance. For the Vikings this primeval substance was fire, which melted other fundamental stuff – ice. For the ancient Hebrews God created the world not from nothingness but from a chaos of earth and water. Only later Christianity introduced the concept of creation *ex nihilo*, apparently to avoid the suggestion that the available building material limited God's creativeness. This conception trickled down to Judaism and Islam, and now all three monotheistic religions admit that our world owes its existence to God and nothing else.

The first naturalistic cosmogonies (i.e. the stories of the creation of the Cosmos) proposed by ancient Greek philosophers similarly trace the origins of the world back to some fundamental stuff. For Thales of Miletus this primeval stuff was water, while Heraclitus of Ephesus saw fire as the source of everything. More sophisticated conceptions include that of Anaximander, who enigmatically described the original substance which the whole world was composed of as "the Boundless". Aristotle, on the other hand, insisted that every object is funded upon formless matter with no intrinsic properties. Aristotle famously rejected the notion of a void, and hence was loath to accept the possibility of the universe coming out of nothing. But his Christian follower, St Thomas Aquinas, had no qualms about admitting that God created the world out of nothing, although he hastened to explain that this claim does not elevate nothingness to the status of being, but merely denies that God created the world out of *something*.

The German polymath, Gottfried Wilhelm Leibniz, explicitly posed the question "Why is there something rather than nothing?" as a legitimate and fundamental metaphysical problem. His Principle of

Sufficient Reason demanded an unequivocal answer to this question, which he predictably found in the concept of God. But how can we find a rational explanation for God's own existence? To this riddle Leibniz offered the following solution: the only reasonable explanation of why God exists is that he is a necessary being. In other words, God's non-existence is logically impossible. This is essentially the *causa sui* explanation for God's existence (God is his own cause and explanation). But Leibniz's conception of necessary beings was seriously undermined by David Hume and Immanuel Kant, who argued that the fact that a given entity exists can never be guaranteed by logic alone. All existential claims, including the one about God, belong to the category of contingent statements, i.e. such that it is possible for them to be false. For Hume the question of why there is something rather than nothing can never be answered, since such an answer cannot be grounded in our experience. Kant, on the other hand, argued for the same conclusion on the basis of his own philosophical system. According to Kant, the notions of causality and time are creations of our own minds and do not have counterparts in the objective world, hence they cannot be used in a satisfactory solution of the puzzle of the world's existence.

Hume and Kant's criticism of the metaphysical riddle of being deeply affected all subsequent thinkers. Some of them chose to ignore both philosophers' admonishments, offering instead drawn-out and winding ponderings on the greatest riddle of being. George Friedrich Hegel, an 18th-century German idealist, wrote pages upon pages full of statements describing how being vanishes into nothing and nothing vanishes into being, but this did not move the problem a bit. Friedrich Schelling, another German thinker of the Romanticism period, insisted that the riddle of being cannot find a rational solution, and that the creation of something out of nothing is incomprehensible. The 20th-century German existentialist, Martin Heidegger, made the notion of nothingness one of the central concepts of his philosophy, but his analysis hardly advanced beyond linguistic divagations on the connections between various synonyms of the term "being" in different languages. The French philosopher Henri Bergson made an honest attempt to seriously attack the problem of why there is something rather than nothing. He argued in a convoluted way that the existence of the world is logically necessary, but his proof did not convince anybody except himself.

A large group of philosophers subscribe to the view that the question of why the universe exists is ultimately meaningless. Ludwig Wittgenstein, one of the most influential philosophers of the 20th century, admitted that the fact that the world exists is one of the greatest metaphysical mysteries. However, it is impossible to properly express this mystery in words, therefore the question of why the world exists is devoid of meaning. The logical positivist Alfred J. Ayer, on the other hand, did not agree that the riddle of being hides any ineffable mysteries in its womb. For him it simply does not make any sense to ask where the whole universe comes from, because the origin itself must be part of the universe. An event which precedes all existing events is impossible, since it would have to precede itself as well. The analytic tradition of philosophy, to which Ayer subscribed, distinguishes two kinds of truths: empirical truths and logical truths. Because logical truths depend solely on the meaning of words, they cannot be used in explanations of facts about reality. Empirical truths, on the other hand, can explain one event only in terms of a different one, hence they are not capable of explaining the universe as a whole. Consequently, the existence of the world turns out to be a brute fact with no scientific explanation. The universe is just there, and that's that.

However, the discovery of the Big Bang makes the question "Why does the world exist?" harder to dodge. To make matters worse, we now have to confront the question of how it is possible that something can come out of nothing. Theologians insist that only God can accomplish such a feat, but the divine act of creation is not exactly creation *ex nihilo*, since God must have already existed before the universe. Quantum mechanics, on the other hand, opens up the possibility of spontaneous tunneling which can account for the transition from nothingness to something.

Generally, philosophers can be divided into three camps with respect to the question "Why is there something rather than nothing?" First there are the optimists who believe that the question admits a meaningful answer, and this answer can be discovered by us. The pessimists admit that the question has an answer, but we will never be able to know for sure. And the rejectionists question the very intelligibility of the problem. The pessimists and the rejectionists may be accused of being too quick to surrender without thoroughly evaluating all possible solutions to the riddle of being.

It may be also observed that the motives for pursuing the mystery of existence are not only intellectual, but emotional ones as well. The world as a whole can elicit two types of emotions: positive and negative. For instance Arthur Schopenhauer and the existentialists frowned upon reality. For them the world is full of suffering and misery, and its existence is ultimately worse than non-existence. The world can also be disgusting and repulsive. Fortunately, the pessimists don't often practice what they preach, and they usually enjoy life's pleasures as any other person.

3 THE POWER OF NOTHING

The Greek philosopher Parmenides issued a dire warning that we should not dare to speak about what is not on the pain of contradiction. Indeed, the word "nothing" can be used as the basis for many logical tricks and word plays, for instance the following seemingly impeccable reasoning: nothing is better than steak, and hamburger is certainly better than nothing, therefore hamburger is better than steak.[3] Speaking more seriously, nothing is often seen as a sinister force. In theology nothing is what God does not will, and therefore must be evil, satanic. Existentialists associated nothingness with dread. Jean-Paul Sartre averred that nothingness haunts being. Heidegger distinguished between fear, which has a specific object, and anxiety, which is more universal. Anxiety is usually caused by the thought of nothingness. But nothingness is not an object for Heidegger. Rather, it is a dynamic, annihilating and destructive force.

Robert Nozick took Heidegger's idea to a new level, and suggested that nothing as a destructive force can eliminate itself, thus giving rise to something. But such metaphors had been severely criticized as meaningless by logical positivists. Rudolf Carnap insisted that we should not treat "nothing" as if it were a noun which referred to something. This error is responsible for numerous paradoxes. As for Parmenides and his rejection of nothingness, logical analysis can help us overcome his troubles by treating the word "nothing" contextually. To illustrate this method: "Nothing is greater than God" should be interpreted as meaning "God is greater than anything else". Thus "nothing" is not a name of an entity which would surpass even God in greatness. In contrast with that, "nothingness" can be interpreted as a name. In the language of set theory the difference between nothing and nothingness can be explicated with the help of the notion of the empty set. The empty set contains no elements, thus it contains nothing. But the empty set itself is something, and therefore it can be equated with nothingness. This can be summarized as follows: nothingness = {nothing}.

Losses, gaps and holes are bits of nothingness, surrounded by a world of being. But absolute nothingness is the total absence of everything. Some say that nothingness is impossible. However, we can clearly imagine it: all we have to do is visualizing the situation in which all objects begin to disappear, one by one. But Henri Bergson objected to this thought experiment. He argued that in order to imagine my consciousness disappearing, I have to invoke another consciousness witnessing this process. Therefore absolute nothingness is conceptually impossible. This argument, supported also by F.H. Bradley, is often called the observer argument. However, we have to beware of the philosopher's fallacy: reasoning from the inability of imagining something that this something is impossible. There are many existing things which we can't imagine – for instance we can't visualize colorless objects, and yet atoms and elementary particles do not have any colors. Furthermore, the observer argument has a dubious consequence that every possible world should contain at least one observer. But a universe without consciousness is surely possible.

Another argument against the intelligibility of nothingness is the container argument. It may be pointed out that there is still something left when we imagine emptiness: it is namely the container, or the abstract setting. The contemporary Oxford philosopher Bede Rundle identifies this container with space itself. We can't think away the presence of space. Yet another argument offered by Rundle goes as follows: if there were nothing, there would be the fact that there is nothing, and therefore there would be something, after all. This argument, however, seems to be based on several fallacies.[4] As for the original argument from the existence of space, it begs the question of whether space is really something. This philosophical problem is debated by two major schools: substantivalism and relationism. Substantivalists believe that space is indeed a substance capable of existing independently from anything it may contain. On the other hand, for relationists space is a mere "reflection" of the relations between physical objects, and when those physical objects vanish, space vanishes too. But if substantivalists are right, then it is possible to imagine a totally empty space. One argument supporting substantivalism is that according to modern science space has certain intrinsic properties – it may be finite, infinite, curved, etc.

Regardless of which of the two positions on the nature of space is closer to the truth, it may be argued that the container argument is invalid. If space is a mere reflection of spatial relations between objects, then it would have to disappear when the physical world disappeared. But if space is a physical substance, we may go one step further, and eliminate it after having eliminated all the material objects contained within it. This elimination may be achieved by first imagining a finite space of a given radius, and then mathematically shrinking this radius to zero.

The procedure of eradicating physical objects in order to achieve a perfect vacuum can be attempted in a laboratory. Aristotle believed that nature abhors vacuum, and therefore will resist any such attempts. However, the Italian physicist Evangelista Torricelli succeeded in creating a tiny airless pocket of space in a glass test tube. But did he create a true bit of emptiness? This may be doubted, as there was certainly a bit of something left inside the tube: some stray gas molecules, radiation, etc. And even a perfect vacuum with no particles inside still contains something, because it possesses the lowest energy level, which can never go to zero. The state of the lowest energy is known as the vacuum state.

Nevertheless, the subtraction argument purports to demonstrate that an absolute void is metaphysically possible. The assumptions on which this argument rests are that the world contains a finite number of objects, and that those objects are contingent (they might not have existed). Yet another premise is the assumption of independence: the nonexistence of one thing does not imply the existence of another thing. With these premises we can prove the possibility of nothingness by eliminating each object one by one. But the independence premise can be questioned. A counterexample to this assumption involves two electrically charged particles. Because charge is conserved, one particle cannot vanish, since that would diminish the total charge of the universe.[5] The moral from this failure is that the transition from being to non-being is not a simple matter, and that at best it can be achieved asymptotically.

Can absolute nothingness be coherently described? Modern logic shows us how to do that. To begin with, "Nothing exists" translates as "For every x, it is not the case that x exists". But "exists" does not name any specific property. It may be argued that existing is characterized as possessing some properties, and therefore the statement describing absolute nothingness could be expressed by saying that no object possesses any property at all. But we don't have an exhaustive list of all properties at our disposal. One solution may be to use a universal property which any object should possess by necessity, such as the property of being identical with itself: $x = x$. In such an interpretation the sentence "Something exists" is translated as "There is an x such that $x = x$". And its negation "There is no x such that $x = x$" supposedly represents the statement that there is nothing at all.

However, we encounter a problem here. The "nihilistic claim" can be reformulated as stating "For all x, it is not true that $x = x$". But it is a logical truth that each object is identical with itself: "For all x, $x = x$". Therefore it looks like the statement that there is nothing is logically impossible. One solution to this problem is to use a system of logic called "free logic" in which an empty universe is admitted. In an empty universe all universal statements become true (because there are no counterexamples which could make them false – they are called vacuously true), and all existential ones become false. In free logic no contradiction can be derived from the assumption that nothing exists.[6] Absolute nothingness is self-consistent.

One crucial feature of the null world (the world which contains nothing) is that it is the simplest of all possible worlds. Simplicity is often held as a sign of truth of probability, and this fact creates an immediate explanatory challenge of why the null hypothesis is not true. The null world is also the least arbitrary and the most symmetrical one, which means that it is invariant under any transformations. Using the fundamental physical concept of entropy we may note that the entropy of nothingness is minimal (that is, zero) because there is only one state of nothingness. While the entropy of our universe increases, the entropy of the null world always stays the same. To conclude, the mystery of existence can be now expressed as follows: why isn't a world which is the simplest, the least arbitrary, the most symmetrical, and has the nicest entropy profile, the actual one?

Adolf Grünbaum is a modern philosopher of science who emphatically rejects the mystery of existence. For him the question of why the world exists rests on some presuppositions – mainly that the world needs an explanation. But is really nothingness a more natural state? Grünbaum attacks the thesis of the Spontaneity of Nothingness – a misguided idea taken from theism, or more specifically from Christianity and its concept of creation *ex nihilo*. For Christians God not only created the universe but also sustains it. Without God the world would slip back into non-existence (this is called the Dependency Axiom). But the Greeks didn't have that problem, because they didn't share the belief in creation ex nihilo.

Empirically, the statement that there is something is the most trivial and uninteresting one. Grünbaum argues that simplicity is not connected with the truth and the objective world, as it is only a psychological concept. Nothingness is not a natural state, since the notion of naturalness is derived from experience, and we don't have an experience of nothingness. However, it may be observed that the idea of nothingness is indirectly derived from experience through our best scientific theory of the universe, i.e. the Big Bang theory, which assumes that the world had a beginning. But Grünbaum replies that this does not entail that there was a time before the universe appeared when there was nothing. Strictly speaking there was no time "before" the Big Bang, so it doesn't make sense to say that the universe came out of nothingness. Even though the universe is temporally finite, it has always existed, meaning that there has never been a moment in which there was no universe. Consequently, there was no violation of the conservation of mass and energy at the point of singularity.

4 FINITE VS. INFINITE

The universe, according to our current knowledge, is temporarily bounded. It started its existence over 14 billion years ago, and most probably will come to an end sometime in the future. It seems that the finitude of the universe makes it less secure in its existence. A universe which has always existed and will never cease to exist makes a more solid appearance. But the notion of an infinite universe is a source of many potential paradoxes and complications. Kant argued that in a world with no beginning it is hard to explain how a given day might have arrived if it had been preceded by an infinite number of earlier days. We can eventually get to any natural number N no matter how big by counting forward starting with 1, 2, up to N, but how can we achieve the same number counting backward from infinity: ... $N+2$, $N+1$, N? Another way of putting this objection is to say that in a world with an infinite past it would have to be possible to finish an infinite series of tasks, which seems to be paradoxical. But if we have an infinite amount of time, finishing an infinite task presents no problem. An infinite series of tasks may even be completed in a finite amount of time if for instance each task takes a shorter amount of time than its predecessor. One example of such an infinite task is for instance ordinary motion, as revealed in the well-known Zeno "paradoxes". In order to move from point A to point B we have to pass through an endless series of motions: first we cover one half of the distance from A to B, then a half of the remaining distance, and so on. But because each distance in the sequence is covered in half the time of its predecessor, the total task can be finished in a finite interval of time.

The concept of a universe with no temporal limits has been supported by many scholars, including Newton and Einstein. Einstein himself faced a problem when his equations yielded a model of an expanding universe. In order to achieve an agreement with the assumption of a static and eternal universe he added an *ad hoc* factor to his equation, which later turned out to be his greatest scientific blunder. But even an expanding universe need not have a beginning. A model of the universe called the Steady State Universe, proposed by Thomas Gold, Hermann Bondi and Fred Hoyle, is both expanding and eternal. This combination of properties is achieved by the assumption that new matter is constantly created to fill the empty space made by escaping galaxies. Another method of reconciling the expansion of the universe with its eternity is provided by the Oscillating Universe model suggested by Alexander Friedmann. According to this hypothesis, the universe goes through periods of expansion and contraction, and the cycle repeats itself forever. Unfortunately, the Steady-State model is inconsistent with astronomical observations, while the Oscillating Universe model is plagued by serious theoretical problems. For now the dominating theoretical model is the Big Bang theory, which assumes that the universe does not stretch indefinitely in the past.

But the standard Big Bang theory is not science's last word. The current theory that best accounts for the Big Bang is the inflationary cosmology, according to which explosions similar to our Big Bang are common occurrences. The new inflationary theory assumes that our universe came into being as part of a vast preexisting universe in which numerous other universes pop into existence in a similar fashion. Thus the idea of an eternal super-universe may be possible to be reconciled with the Big Bang after all.

Hume gave two arguments for the claim that an eternal world does not require an explanation for its existence. The first argument states that because a causal explanation must involve a cause which precedes a given event, no explanation can be offered for an eternal world, since no cause can precede it.[7] The second argument, in turn, points out that in a world which has no beginning every event can be potentially explained by an earlier occurrence. If each event has its own cause, we don't need any further explanation for the totality of events which constitute the entire world. The demand for such an explanation is unreasonable. This argument may be interpreted as implying that in a sense an eternal universe is its own cause.[8]

But the notion of *causa sui* is in itself deeply problematic. An infinite series of copies of the same book can be "explained" by pointing out that each copy in the series is a replica of the previous one. But does this truly explain where the entire book came from? Another example of that sort can be produced using the concept of a time machine. Suppose that a visitor from the future (who may be just your old self) comes to your house and hands you plans of how to build a time machine. You follow the instructions and create such a machine which enables you (or someone else) to go back in time and carry the plans to your younger self, so that the circle is closed now. Even though each element in the loop is causally explained by its own cause (the plans of the time machine you get come from the future, while the future plans you carry from the past), still the fundamental question "Who (or what) created the plans of the time machine?" remains unanswered.

Another controversial point regarding the explanation of an eternal universe in terms of an infinite causal chain is related to the concept of the laws of nature. In order to causally explain a given occurrence in terms of an earlier cause we need to apply a law which can predict the later occurrence given the earlier state of the system. For instance, the value of the total mass-energy of the universe at this very moment can be explained by saying that the same value characterized the universe an hour earlier, and the law of the conservation of mass-energy implies that this value must stay unchanged. But now we can ask for an explanation of the law of conservation, so the business of explaining the entire universe together with its laws is not finished yet.

5 A THEOLOGICAL EXPLANATION OF THE WORLD

Richard Swinburne is a philosopher and theologian from the University of Oxford. He is particularly well known to the general public from his heated debates with the fellow Oxonian and avowed atheist, Richard Dawkins. Swinburne admits that the fact that the world exists is a deep mystery in need for an explanation, especially because of the tremendous complexity and richness of the actual universe. For him the God hypothesis gives us the simplest explanation for the existence of such a complex world. Swinburne's reasoning is based on the methodological principle (rejected by Grünbaum) that the simplest explanations are most likely to be true. The principle of simplicity is commonly used in everyday life, as without it we would be hard pressed to make sense of what we observe around us (we can always contrive many alternative hypotheses explaining the same observed facts, but we have to choose only one such hypothesis). Whether the universe had a finite or an infinite past does not matter to the riddle of existence: either way the universe stands in need for an explanation, and the best explanation available is the one based on the notion of God.

It is particularly striking that our universe is so well suited to host life. If some fundamental constants were slightly different from what they actually are, no biochemistry and consequently no organic life would be possible. For Swinburne the simplest explanation for this fact is that God personally tuned all the necessary parameters for the occurrence of life and consciousness. But there is an alternative explanation of this amazing coincidence which has the potential to make this coincidence look quite unremarkable. This explanation assumes that our universe is just one of a multitude of different universes, each characterized by different initial conditions. While the vast majority of these universes can't possibly harbor life, some of them are bound to have just the right conditions, and our universe by necessity belongs to this small category (because we are here rather than anywhere else).

Swinburne's reply to this argument (the argument is often referred to as the anthropic principle) is that the multiverse hypothesis is unnecessarily complicated. It postulates a myriad of universes which can't be accessed by us. Moreover, this hypothesis has to presuppose some laws which govern the way separate universes with different initial conditions are created. But what can explain the existence of these laws? Why is the multiverse the way it (presumably) is, as opposed to any other possible arrangement? For Swinburne the hypothesis of a divine creator is much simpler, and therefore it should be preferred.

But is it really simpler? One objection to Swinburne's view may be that the God hypothesis is not that simple, since God himself must be an enormously complex entity. God acts for a purpose, makes decisions, and holds beliefs. Doesn't this require a mind which is at least as complex as a human mind? In fact, the level of complexity of God's mind should infinitely surpass the degree of complexity of our minds, since God is omniscient, and hence possesses a knowledge of every minute detail of the universe. Because of that, God's internal complexity should be at least equal to that of the world. Swinburne tries to downplay this problem by arguing first that the complexity of the human mind stems from the fact that it is inextricably connected with the brain with its intricate neurological structure, whereas God is a pure spirit and does not require a material substratum. Moreover, Swinburne observes that in science we often postulate kinds of "infinite" powers similar to those which are usually attributed to God. For instance, gravitational force is such a power, since two objects interact gravitationally regardless of how far away from each other they are. So the God hypothesis is no more complex than ordinary scientific hypotheses.

Another important challenge for theists of the Swinburne type is how to explain why God is the heavenly-father figure as portrayed by Christianity, and not a deistic maker of the universe, or even an abstract universal principle. If the main reason why we adopt the God hypothesis is that it is the simplest theory which explains the existence and complexity of the universe, then all we need is a divine creator who walks away from the world the moment it is brought into being. Why would such a God intervene in our lives or listen to our prayers? Swinburne's answer to these worries is that God keeps a connection with his own creation because of his infinite goodness.[9] In response to the well-known problem of evil, Swinburne offers his preferred version of theodicy, that is a defense of God's goodness. In essence, suffering is a result of the existence of free will. God wants us to be free, so he must allow that we sometimes may do evil things.

Many philosophers hold that God's existence is necessary. But Swinburne disagrees with that. For him a world with no God is conceivable. However, God is a necessary being in the sense that he does not depend for his existence on anything else. God's existence cannot be further explained – it is a brute fact. Thus the God hypothesis does not fully resolve the mystery of being, as it answers one question ("Why does the world exist?") at the price of introducing another ("Why does God exist?").

Swinburne's main argument for the God hypothesis is that it is the simplest explanation of the mystery of being. But philosophers and theologians have offered dozens of other proofs for God's existence. One traditional way to argue for the existence of a supreme being is known as the cosmological argument. This reasoning, which can be traced back to Aristotle, is based on the premise that the existence of the world is contingent, i.e. that the world might not very well have come into being. Hence its existence requires a cause or explanation. But if the cause of the world is itself contingent, it stands in need of a similar explanation. Thus clearly there must be a necessary being that causally explains the universe. And the existence of such a necessary being is self-explanatory. It only remains to show that this being possesses typical attributes associated with God, such as infinite power and intelligence.

Clearly the cosmological argument is based on two crucial premises. One of them, close in spirit to Leibniz's Principle of Sufficient Reason, states that everything has a causal explanation. The other one is the assumption that the world is contingent. Both seem to be derivable from experience (in particular, the contingency assumption can be inferred from the observed fact that material things do not last forever). But one may wonder whether the existence of a necessary being shouldn't be provable using only a priori assumptions independent from experience. This goal is purportedly achieved in the so-called ontological argument for God's existence. This argument, originally formulated by an 11th-century monk Anselm, starts with the unquestionable assumption that God should be defined as the greatest being possible, that is a being such that nothing greater can even be conceived. This definition should be acceptable regardless of whether one believes in God or not, for this is just how we are supposed to understand the term "God". In a similar vein, one can accept the definition of Santa Claus "the jolly bearded man clad in red who rides a reindeer-drawn sleigh and gives presents on Christmas" without actually admitting that Santa exists.

But for Anselm the definition of God is special in that it alone can guarantee the necessary existence of God. To show that this is the case, Anselm accepts one more a priori premise: that existence is more perfect than non-existence. And now we can reason that if God did not exist, he would not be the greatest being imaginable, for we could imagine an even greater being, namely a God that is real as opposed to being imaginary. Thus the very definition of God apparently forces us to accept his existence. This reasoning can be presented succinctly as follows:

Premise 1. God is the greatest conceivable being.
Premise 2. A being that exists is greater than the same being which is only imaginary.
Intermediary conclusion: If God didn't exist (i.e. if he were imaginary), he would not be the greatest conceivable being.
Final conclusion: God must exist.

This argument has been criticized on many counts. The most famous attack on the ontological argument came from Kant, who argued that existence cannot be treated on a par with other characteristics typically used in definitions. In short, existence is not a property which can differentiate between various entities. When we say that God does not exist, we don't want to claim that he lacks one property – existence – while retaining all the other properties. There is simply no non-existent God. According to modern logic, the definition of God (and any other concept, for that matter) should be properly built in the form of a logical equivalence:

x is a God if and only if x is such that no other object can be conceived to be greater than x.

The crucial fact about the above-written formula is that it remains true even if there is no x which satisfies the condition formulated in the definition (logicians explain this by pointing out that the equivalence of two false statements is still true). Consequently, the atheist can accept God's definition without accepting the statement that God is really the greatest conceivable being. Instead, the atheist should only accept the conditional statement that *if* God existed, he by definition would be the greatest conceivable being. So Anselm can only prove that it is true that if God existed, he would have to exist, which is a trivial fact.

However, modern logic offers a surprising new possibility of revamping the old Anselmian trick. A new version of the ontological proof has been developed within the framework of so-called modal logic, i.e. logic that formalizes the concepts of necessity and possibility. Among the champions of the modal version of Anselm's argument are the famous logician and mathematician Kurt Gödel, and the contemporary philosopher and logician Alvin Plantinga. The gist of this new argument is that the notion of God should include an even stronger assertion of greatness than the one assumed by Anselm. God should not only be defined as the greatest being, but his greatness should be also necessary and not merely accidental. This postulate can be expressed in the condition that if God exists at all, he exists necessarily (we can call this property of God "maximal greatness"). In modal logic the notion of necessity and its complementary concept of possibility are defined as follows: a statement is necessarily true if it is true in all possible worlds, and is possibly true, if it is true in some possible worlds. Thus, by definition, if God exists in any possible world, he should exist in all possible worlds.

But now it can be argued that because the definition of God given above does not contain any logical inconsistency, there should be at least one possible world in which a being defined in such a way exists. This looks like a reasonable way of thinking. For instance, there seems to be no logical contradiction in the notion of the first-born son of Elisabeth I, Queen of England. Even though Elisabeth in fact died childless, she might have had a son, and therefore there is a possible world in which her son does exist. However, when we apply the same reasoning to the notion of the maximally greatest God, we can notice that from his definition it follows that because he exists in one possible world, he must exist in all possible worlds, including our world. Thus the existence of God seems to be proven.

However, the theists' victory is not secure yet. It may be observed that a similar argument can be produced in favor of the exactly opposite conclusion: that God cannot exist in any possible world. As the supposition of the non-existence of the maximally greatest being does not seem to involve a direct logical contradiction, it should be true in at least one possible world. But if the maximally greatest God does not exist in one possible world, he must be absent from any other possible world. It looks like equally compelling arguments can be produced in favor of two opposing claims: that God exists in all possible worlds, and that God is absent from all possible worlds. Logic can prove that the maximally greatest being either necessarily exists or necessarily does not exist, but is unable to tell us which is the case. And this should not surprise us, for it would be truly astounding if armchair divagations regarding pure rational thought (which is what logic ultimately comes down to) could produce an important truth about the real world.

6 PHYSICS AND THE MULTIVERSE

David Deutsch is a contemporary theoretical physicist whose main achievements include the development of the idea of a universal quantum computer. He is also known as a staunch supporter of the many-worlds interpretation of quantum mechanics, which leads directly to one version of the multiverse hypothesis. The many-worlds interpretation was originally proposed and developed by Hugh Everett III, and is also known as the Everettian interpretation of quantum mechanics. This conception attempts to solve the perennial problem of quantum measurement. According to the fundamental postulates of the quantum theory, the initial state of a quantum system gives us only the probabilities of future results of experiments, rather than the exact values of all relevant physical parameters. Quantum measurements do not reveal preexisting properties but in a sense create them out of numerous possibilities. But this can hardly be reconciled with the fact that all quantum-mechanical interactions should obey the deterministic law of evolution encompassed in the so-called Schrödinger equation. The many-worlds interpretation solves this problem by assuming that at the moment of measurement the world splits into as many copies as there are possible outcomes of this measurement having non-zero probability. In the famous example of the Schrödinger cat there are two possible results of the experiment: dead cat or alive cat. Thus there are two copies of the same world: one in which the cat is dead, and the other where the cat is not dead.

Different worlds which arise as a result of measurement-type interactions are parallel to each other, which means that they contain slightly different variants of the same entities (for instance the same cat is dead in one world but alive in another). The many worlds are also causally isolated: no known physical interaction can connect them, and therefore I can't communicate with my copy that observes the dead cat while I look at the alive variant. The number of alternative realities postulated by the Everettian interpretation is huge, as the numbers of potential outcomes of typical measurements are enormous (in some cases they are even infinite).

The many-worlds interpretation of quantum mechanics is not the only route to the conception of a multiverse. Another impulse to postulate numerous universes other than our own can come from experience. Measurements of the cosmic background radiation suggest that the space we inhabit is infinite and that all matter is distributed randomly in it. From this it can be inferred that all possible arrangements of matter should exist in some parts of this infinite universe. And because of the vast distances between various such arrangements and the finite speed at which light travels, such arrangements are effectively like separate universes. Moreover, the laws of probability dictate that each of us should have numerous copies in other universes.

Another scientific idea that can give rise to the multiverse hypothesis is the so-called chaotic inflation theory postulated by the physicist Andrei Linde. This theory implies that Big Bang type events should be fairly common, and therefore there should be a multitude of separate universes popping into existence in some primordial megauniverse. The idea of many parallel universes can not only help us solve conceptual problems in the foundations of quantum mechanics, but can also shed new light on the explanation of the existence of life in our universe based on the anthropic principle. It is a well-known fact that perfect conditions are necessary to make organic life possible in our universe. The laws of nature and its fundamental constants have to be such that complex organic chemistry could have a chance to occur. On top of that, the specific physical conditions on a life-bearing planet have to precisely fall within a very narrow margin (the so-called Goldilocks zone: not too hot and not too cold). The multiverse hypothesis can explain the fact that life appeared in our universe by pointing out that however small the probability of such an event is, statistically it is bound to happen in some universe given their enormous number.[10]

But can the hypothesis of a multiverse help us in our quest for the ultimate explanation of the mystery of existence? David Deutsch is skeptical. For him no ultimate explanation of the existence of the entire multiverse is possible. We can only produce better and better explanations of some aspects of reality, but there will always be something left out. For instance, quantum mechanics cannot account for the creation of something out of nothing. Even though the process of the creation of a pair of a particle and its antiparticle in a vacuum (the reversal of the annihilation process) is admissible according to the laws of quantum physics, this is not yet *creatio ex nihilo*, since the vacuum is not exactly empty (it contains some background energy). Actually, the existence of absolute emptiness is prohibited by the laws of quantum mechanics, in particular Heisenberg's uncertainty principle. The uncertainty principle forbids the existence of systems for which certain pairs of measurable properties would simultaneously take precise, well-defined values. For instance, it is impossible to create a quantum system whose position and momentum (velocity times mass) would be precisely defined. If we wanted to measure the position of a particle with an arbitrarily high degree of precision, the value of its velocity would become completely undefined (and vice versa).

Another pair of mutually incompatible observables characterizing a physical field consists of the value (or intensity) of this field and the rate at which it changes. Due to Heisenberg's uncertainty relation, a field whose value is zero everywhere is impossible, since both the value of the field and the rate of its change would have to take precise values, namely zero. This fact is interpreted by some physicists as showing that a true vacuum is unstable, as it immediately tends to create something so that Heisenberg's principle of uncertainty can be satisfied. But how can we imagine true emptiness? Even empty space which has no field in it has certain spatiotemporal properties – its "fabric" can be twisted or curved. The mathematical idea of sheer nothingness has been worked out by the Ukrainian physicist Alex Vilenkin. He suggested describing nothingness as the result of shrinking a closed spacetime to the point of zero radius. Using the principles of quantum theory, Vilenkin was able to show that an energy-carrying vacuum can spontaneously arise out of this sheer nothingness through the process of tunneling.[11] In the second stage of this process the tiny amount of energetic vacuum rapidly expands thanks to the process of inflation. Both stages of the hypothetical process leading from nothing to something are supported by well-confirmed scientific theories: quantum mechanics and the theory of inflation.

However, the transition from the absolute state of nothingness to something (even though this something is initially only a tiny bit of vacuum) remains a mysterious event. It is even hard to describe this happening as an event, since events occur in time, and there is no time unless there is *something*. Another problem is the existence of laws which supposedly govern the transition from nothing to something. Laws are clearly something, so doesn't the reference to laws violate the assumption of sheer nothingness?

Steven Weinberg, one of the most famous living physicists and a Nobel Prize laureate, is rather skeptical about the possibility of the ultimate explanation of the world's existence. For him, even if the laws of nature dictated that there must be something, or that nothingness is unstable, still the question "Why are the laws one way rather than another?" would remain. Weinberg also believes that current physics can offer us little help in the task of explaining the origin of the universe. In the extreme conditions of high density and temperature around the Big Bang all known theories, including general relativity, break down. Even Hawking's theorems about singularities have limited applicability in this situation. Rather than attempting in vain to tackle the mystery of existence, we should focus our efforts on answering the question "Why are things the way they are?". This is what drives the scientists who are pursuing the final theory of physics. Such a theory should give an account of everything that happens in the universe, including its initial conditions. But even such an all-encompassing theory will not be capable of explaining its own existence. The question "Why are the laws as described by the (as of yet unknown) final theory?" will remain unanswered.

Weinberg agrees that the idea of a multiverse can dissolve the mystery of life and consciousness in our universe by appealing to the anthropic principle. But the multiverse theory cannot solve all philosophical problems. The mystery of why the laws of nature are such that they enable the existence of a myriad of alternative universes remains unexplained. Still, the concept of a multiverse has some obvious theoretical advantages. One way of deriving the multiverse hypothesis is through the application of string theory. String theory constitutes an attempt to unify all known physical phenomena and interactions into one cohesive whole. Because the equations of string theory have an enormous number of different solutions, these solutions can be interpreted as representing various alternative realities. String theorists invoke here the concept of the Landscape, which contains a vast array of "pocket universes", each instantiating a different solution to the equations. These universes can differ radically from each other with respect to their dimensionality, the types of elementary particles and fundamental interactions, and so on. Only a few of the universes allowed by the equations of string theory could possibly support life.

All ultimate explanations of the mystery of existence based on laws are open to the objection that the laws themselves are part of reality to be explained, and therefore require an additional explanation. Laws are just patterns of regularities occurring in the worlds. It may turn out that the laws describing regularities inside the world are incompatible with the non-existence of this world. But the explanation of the world's existence given with the help of such laws seems circular. In order to accept the laws, we have to presuppose the existence of the world which displays the required regularities. The patterns observed in the world cannot properly explain the existence of this very world.[12]

7 MATHEMATICS AND THE REAL WORLD

Given the apparent lack of success in the quest for a scientific explanation of the mystery of existence, it may be suggested that we should turn to mathematics for help. Perhaps some fundamental mathematical principles or concepts could provide us with the sought-after explanation of why there is something rather than nothing. Mathematics has always been at the center of philosophical considerations. The Greek mathematician and philosopher Pythagoras believed that our world is literally made of numbers. Plato, on the other hand, insisted that mathematical objects exist in a realm separate from the material world. This realm of mathematical objects is known as the world of ideas, or Platonic heaven. Today the majority of mathematicians can be classified as Platonists, which means that they believe in the objective and mind-independent existence of non-spatiotemporal mathematical objects. One of the staunchest Platonists was the great mathematician and logician Kurt Gödel. He claimed that we could have a direct contact with the world of abstract mathematical entities with the help of the faculty of our minds he called mathematical intuition.

Apart from the two major philosophical questions "What are mathematical objects?" and "How can we have any knowledge about abstract, mathematical entities?", there is yet another thorny issue worth mentioning here. This is namely the problem of the incredible or even unreasonable effectiveness of mathematics in the natural sciences. Why should abstract objects which exist outside space and time have any clout in the physical world? And yet some mathematicians and scientists argue in a somewhat Pythagorean fashion that the physical world is ultimately mathematical in nature. One of these scientists is sir Roger Penrose, an eminent Oxford physicist and mathematician. Penrose gained international fame for his brilliant mathematical work on black holes and the concept of singularity, as well as on twistor theory and the unification of quantum mechanics with general relativity. His philosophical views are uncompromisingly Platonic, or even Pythagorean. On the basis of Gödel's incompleteness theorem Penrose argues that the human mind is capable of making mathematical discoveries that are beyond reach of even the most powerful computers.[13] The power of the human mind requires quantum mechanics to operate, or even an as-of-yet not discovered theory of quantum gravity.

Penrose's main metaphysical hypothesis is that there are three distinct but connected worlds: the physical world of material bodies, the Platonic world of mathematical objects, and the world of mental states, or conscious thoughts.[14] These three worlds are not independent from one another, although their mutual interconnections are quite mysterious. The mental world of conscious awareness arises out of the complex physical structure of the brain. The link between the material and the Platonic worlds is visible in the fact that our best theories explaining the workings of the physical world are written in a mathematical language. And the connection between the mental and the mathematical worlds is established by the direct epistemic access we have to the Platonic realm of mathematics. Although some naturalistically-oriented philosophers question this last connection on the basis of the assumption that an epistemic contact requires a causal interaction between the perceiving subject and the perceived object, Penrose brushes this objection aside, claiming that our direct access to the world of mathematics is unquestionable.

Explaining further the interrelations between the three worlds, Penrose observes that not only does each world emerge out of a tiny bit of one of the other worlds, but, more importantly, this bit also happens to be the most perfect element of the world it belongs to. For instance, the world of consciousness emerges from the brain which is the most complex structure of the known world, much more intricate than stars and galaxies. Similarly, the part of consciousness responsible for mathematical thinking is relatively small, but it is arguably the most perfect and purest part of all conscious thoughts. And the part of mathematics that finds its applications in the description of the physical world is likewise made up of the most sublime mathematical concepts. In Penrose's grand scheme of things the Platonic world spawns the physical worlds through mathematics, the physical world engenders the mental world through the complexity of brain neurochemistry, and the world of consciousness gives rise to the Platonic world through mathematical intuition. But Penrose's three worlds are not equal. Clearly the world of mathematical objects is fundamental, whereas the remaining two are its mere shadows.

Can Penrose's conception be used to solve the riddle of being? The main problem with this approach is that we have to find a firm foundation for the existence of the Platonic world first, in order to further support the material and mental worlds. It seems that Penrose presupposes that the existence of the world of mathematical objects is a logical necessity. It is indeed quite common in philosophy to accept that mathematical statements are necessarily true. Clearly, the statement that 2 plus 2 equals 4 could not possibly fail to be true. So it seems that the statements regarding the existence of mathematical objects should be likewise true by necessity. But things are not that simple. It may be argued that actually no mathematical theorem asserts categorically that mathematical objects exist. Mathematical propositions can be construed as making conditional statements of the "if-then" form. If natural numbers exist, then certainly 2 plus 2 must equal 4. But arithmetic cannot in itself guarantee the existence of numbers. Some philosophers even go as far as to claim that mathematicians routinely dabble in fictions. Mathematicians counteract that accusation by saying that they have a distinct feeling of reality when solving mathematical problems. But why should we take this feeling seriously? For instance Bertrand Russell in his late years admitted that the view that mathematics reveals some transcendental truths is nonsense, and that mathematical statements are simply tautologies.

Recently one particular strategy to defend the objective existence of mathematical objects gained popularity. This strategy is based on the observation that numerous mathematical concepts and principles constitute parts of our best empirical theories, and that it seems that their role in those theories is indispensable. After all, it is hard to imagine any advanced theory in contemporary physics which would not employ some mathematical machinery. The so-called Indispensability Argument (formulated independently by the American philosophers W.V.O. Quine and Hilary Putnam) states that because our empirical theories are well confirmed by experience, this confirmation also "spills over" to the mathematical objects and theorems that are used in these theories. In other words, it is claimed that the existence of mathematical objects is supported by the empirical data which confirm our best scientific theories.

However, the strategy offered by the Indispensability Argument is of little help to the Platonists like Penrose who want to solve the mystery of being by relying on the immutable and perfect world of mathematical objects. According to the Indispensability Argument mathematical entities are just theoretical posits which help us explain observable facts. But if mathematics is to be taken as the foundation of the existence of the physical world, the existence of mathematical entities cannot depend in turn on contingent facts derived from our experience of physical reality. To make matters worse, the claim that mathematics is indeed indispensable in empirical sciences can be legitimately questioned. Hartry Field, a contemporary American philosopher, showed in his provocative book *Science without Numbers* that mathematical vocabulary can be eliminated from the language of selected physical theories if we add some extra physical notions to those theories. According to Field, mathematics plays an extremely useful role in physics by simplifying the way we derive conclusions about the physical world from observational premises, but ultimately in empirical sciences we are only interested in those premises and conclusions, so we can treat the mathematical machinery as scaffolding which in the end can be discarded. While Field's conception is not without its problems, it shows that the Indispensability Argument is not powerful enough to help the Platonist cause.

8 THE DE-MATERIALIZATION OF THE WORLD AND CONSCIOUSNESS

The philosophical discussions on Platonism invite us to take a broader look at the issue of the ultimate nature of reality. Traditionally, this topic belongs to the branch of philosophy known as metaphysics (or ontology). The Greek philosopher Aristotle introduced the concept of metaphysics understood as the most general science about being. Aristotle also held the view (known as hylomorphism) that each object consists of two constitutive elements: matter and form. The matter of a given thing is the stuff it is made of, while its form contains all its properties. It seems that both matter and form are required to work together for an object to come into being. Without the "stuff" reality would be a ghostly combination of mere properties – a structure with nothing to hang on to. On the other hand, unstructurized matter would be like a homogenous and uniform mass with no discerning qualities. And yet over the centuries our views have clearly evolved in the direction of the de-materialization of reality.

Starting with Newton and Faraday, the idea of a field of forces began to emerge in physics. Gravitational and electromagnetic fields were considered an addition to material objects which enabled them to interact at a distance. However, soon it became apparent that the very property of being material owes its reality to those fields. The hallmark of material things is their impenetrability. But modern physics teaches us that impenetrability and sturdiness of matter is a result of an action of two abstract, mathematical principles: Pauli's exclusion principle and Heisenberg's uncertainty principle.[15] Furthermore, fundamental properties of basic constituents of physical reality, such as electrons, do not tell us anything about the intrinsic nature of these objects. For instance mass is just a propensity to accelerate when acted upon by a force, and electric charge is a disposition to interact with electric fields in a certain way. Thus reality seems to reduce to a web of relations with no genuine and independent objects to be connected by these relations. The view that entities participating in a given relational structure do not have any intrinsic character independent from the structure is commonly referred to as structuralism. Structuralism is a popular doctrine in many seemingly unrelated areas of research, from linguistics to mathematics. For instance, mathematicians consider systems which are structurally the same (such systems are called "isomorphic") as essentially one and the same structure. The differences between the objects that constitute distinct exemplifications of a given structure do not matter.

A different but related conception of a reality devoid of any substance sees information as the primary stuff of things. This suggestion is wittily summed up by John Wheeler as "it from bit". This conception assumes that states of the universe are just pure information states characterizing differences between various phenomena. The world is just a constant flow of information without any tangible substance. This radical idea leads naturally to the even more astonishing suggestion that our world may be just a huge computer simulation without any actual computer. For the physicist Frank Tipler the world is only software with no hardware. Even though we may be just simulations, we would never be able to recognize that the world around us is merely an illusion.

However, one key element of reality which may resist the reductionist efforts is our consciousness. Some philosophers, including Thomas Nagel, believe that individual subjective experiences, known as qualia, cannot be fully characterized in terms of objective scientific relations. One argument supporting this stance was formulated by Frank Jackson, an Australian philosopher (the argument is commonly known as the black and white Mary case). Imagine a neuroscientist named Mary who knows everything there is to know about the neurophysiology of color perception. In particular, she knows precisely what neurological processes take place in the brain of a person who sees a red object. And yet Mary has lived for her entire life in a black and white environment, so she has never had a chance to see what red really looks like. This means that there is one vital piece of data about the color red which cannot be reduced to the facts about the neurophysiological states of the brain – it is namely the subjective experience of redness.

Since the time of Alan Turing's seminal paper about Artificial Intelligence (in which he introduced his famous test known as Turing's test) it has been commonly assumed that our minds are just powerful computers, capable of processing phenomenally large amounts of data in short periods of time. But is consciousness fully reducible to computer programs? The philosopher John Searle came up with an argument to the contrary. Imagine a person who does not speak Chinese locked in a room. The person receives strings of Chinese characters, and uses a complicated manual book which tells her what strings of characters to produce back. As it happens, both input and output characters are meaningful sentences written in Chinese, but the person has no idea what they mean. Thus although she follows a program which enables Chinese-speaking people to communicate with her (and, therefore, she is capable of passing the Turing test for being a Chinese speaker), ultimately she does not understand Chinese.

Some naturalistically-oriented philosophers and scientists like Daniel Dennett question the existence of inner, private qualia. For Dennett if something cannot be described in an objective, scientific language, it simply does not exist. But philosophers from Thomas Nagel's camp do not give up easily, throwing in an argument from the privileged access to our conscious states and hence their indubitability. Some of them even go on the offensive, and propose a highly controversial theory known as panpsychism. According to its supporter David Chalmers, consciousness is a much more widespread phenomenon than we usually think. Consciousness does not emerge mysteriously when matter reaches the required level of complexity, as is commonly thought. Instead, as panpsychism alleges, all material objects from elementary particles to clusters of galaxies are endowed with some type of consciousness. The consciousness associated with our brains is just the sum of all consciousnesses of the particles which the brain is made of.

Panpsychism may seem a bit silly and naïve (do electrons really have tiny minds?), but its proponents argue that it solves the almost intractable philosophical problem of the relationship between unconscious matter and the mind. However, the main problem that panpsychism faces is that for now it is incapable of explaining how the individual micro-minds can give rise to one complex mind. Why does each of us have one unified mind instead of a million individual and separated minds? Some philosophers and physicists, including Roger Penrose, look for an answer to this question in the mind-boggling laws of quantum mechanics, in particular those that involve the notion of entangled systems which seem to defy the principle of locality. But for now an attempt to explain consciousness as a quantum-mechanical phenomenon is little more than speculation.

9 FROM GOODNESS TO EXISTENCE

There is one strategy of explaining the puzzle of existence which is radically different from the ones we have discussed so far. Instead of looking for a scientific or mathematical reason for why there is something rather than nothing, we can turn to ethics for possible answers. The central idea of this new approach is that the existence of the world can be explained by the fact that existence is ethically better than non-existence. The ethical need for a good universe is sufficient to create it out of nothingness. A similar idea was contemplated by Plato who argued that the idea of Goodness bestows existence upon all the other ideas. A modern proponent of this metaphysical theory is the English cosmologist and philosopher John Leslie, currently residing in Canada. Leslie refers to his position as "extreme axiarchism" (from the Greek word *axia* meaning "value"). For him there is an objective, metaphysical need for a good universe, and our universe satisfies this need.

Leslie's controversial doctrine is based on the assumption that the cosmos contains an infinite number of infinitely powerful and omniscient minds. Our universe is a contemplative product of one of these minds. But there are numerous other universes being thought of by these minds. While our world does not seem to display particularly high qualities of goodness and perfection, overall the infinite system of many worlds is the most valuable reality, since it contains a variety of possibilities ranging from the universes where the good barely outweighs the evil to the most perfect universes. The existence of "imperfections" and "blemishes" in our world is explained by drawing an analogy with a museum which should have on display not only priceless artworks but also objects of lesser value, because they add to the greater variety.

One problem that such a theory immediately faces is how to prove that goodness has the tendency to be fulfilled. Why should we believe that "ought to exist" implies "does exist"? There are many things that are objectively needed – food for starving children comes to mind first – and yet these things don't materialize themselves as a result of the "ethical requirement" for existence. The connection between goodness and existence is certainly not a logical one, and yet philosophers like Leslie insist it is necessary. That an ethical need is a creative force is a bare and fundamental fact which cannot be further analyzed. If there is no negative force which would oppose any attempt to bring the world into existence, the ethical value of the existing world might be just enough to make its creation happen.

As the philosopher John Mackie observed, the strength of Leslie's conception lies in the fact that it avoids explaining the existence of the world in terms of a first cause. The puzzle of existence cannot be solved by postulating an ultimate cause of everything, be it a physical event or a supernatural God, because the first cause itself requires a further explanation. But Leslie's explanation is not a causal one. The need for goodness is a fact, not a cause. It produces a reason for existence, and a contentious one at that. Mackie ultimately rejects Leslie's explanation, because he remains unconvinced that the ethical value of something can bring it into existence. Answering some of his critics, who wish to see supporting evidence for his claim, Leslie points out that the very existence of the world gives us excellent evidence for his theory. But this reasoning seems circular. Leslie's hypothesis is supposed to explain the world's existence, but we need some independent evidence that the hypothesis holds water. The fact explained by a given hypothesis cannot at the same time serve as evidence in its favor.

As can be seen from this brief overview, Leslie's conception of the ethical explanation for the existence of the world rests on three hidden assumptions. The first assumption is that goodness is an objective property of things which can be possessed independently of people's views and opinions. The second necessary presupposition is the already discussed hypothesis that the goodness of the world is sufficient to bring the world into existence without any intermediate mechanism. And the third required precondition is that our world is indeed ethically valuable to a degree which justifies an appeal to the creative force of goodness. As it seems, all three assumptions are highly controversial. The objective character of ethical values is a hotly debated philosophical issue. Some skeptically-inclined philosophers, like Hume, tend to think that our judgments of right and wrong simply express our subjective emotions. It is doubtful that ethical values would still exist even if all sentient beings disappeared.

But even if objective moral truths and values really existed, how could they create something out of nothing? Insisting that there is an objective moral reason for the world to exist is similar to claiming that the world has a purpose. But purposes without acting agents seem to take us back to the discredited Aristotelian teleology. Finally, the third assumption on which the whole theory of the ethical requiredness of the world rests is even harder to defend than the previous two. To support it we would have to be able to argue not only that the entire multiverse is better than nothingness, but that it is maximally good – better than any conceivable alternative. One of the few philosophers who made a similar claim was Leibniz with his concept of the best of all possible worlds, and for that he was mercilessly pounded by his opponents, including Voltaire. The existence of evil in our world seems to be unquestionable, and various attempts to deal with this problem, such as redefining evil as a mere lack of good or arguing that evil brings harmony to the world, are unconvincing. Leslie's grand vision of the world is optimistic, but this optimism does not appeal to everyone. Some pessimistically-inclined philosophers are drawn to the opposite view that non-existence can actually be better than existence due to the unavoidable suffering associated with the latter.

10 POSSIBILITIES AND SELECTORS

Derek Parfit is a renowned Oxford philosopher, famous for his innovative work on the notion of personal identity. After thoroughly discussing several tricky cases of real and imaginary brain surgeries, he came to the radical conclusion that personal identity and survival don't really matter, and that the concept of the self is an illusion. Parfit's approach to the mystery of being is no less revolutionary. His starting point is the distinction between 'local' and 'cosmic' possibilities. Local possible worlds are universes that exist parallel with our own world, even though they can't be accessed by us. Cosmic possibilities, on the other hand, are the different ways the whole reality (including various local possibilities) might be. Only one such cosmic possibility is actual, and this is what we call our own universe. The difference between local and cosmic possibilities can be best explained with the following example. One cosmic possibility is the null world: a world which does not contain anything. However, there can be no null local possibility. Nothingness cannot exist alongside our world. To add nothing to an existing universe is to do nothing at all.

The null possible world is only one of many cosmic possibilities. Another one, lying at the other extreme, is the fullest possibility called "All Worlds", which contains all conceivable situations. Yet another possibility is that only ethically good worlds exist. But the main question now is which of these cosmic possibilities actually obtains, and why. Parfit calls the special feature that the actually obtaining possibility possesses "the Selector". The Selector is in a sense responsible for the choice of this rather than any other possibility. For instance, if the Selector were the property of simplicity, then the actual world would be the simplest one possible – most probably this would be the Null world, since nothingness seems to be the simplest possibility of all. Goodness as the Selector would result in the best possible world being chosen as the actual one. And if the Selector happened to be the property of being the least arbitrary world, then the All Worlds possibility would be chosen, because there is no arbitrariness in the world which contains all local possibilities with no exception.

However, we don't know which selector is actually in operation, or even if there is any at all. And even if we knew the Selector, we could then ask the question "Why was this selector chosen from among all the possibilities?". It seems that cosmic explanation does not stop at the Selector level but has to be taken one step further. We need a meta-Selector which can operate on the set of all potential selectors. And perhaps we also need meta-meta-Selectors and even higher levels. In order to avoid an infinite regress we can either accept one level's choice as a brute fact without an explanation, or we can try to argue that one selector can actually select itself. The last option may seem plausible, since for instance the criterion of goodness can be used as a selector not only to pick out the best cosmic possibility, but perhaps also to choose itself as the best option among all potential selectors. And yet Parfit rejects this suggestion, arguing that no selector can pick out itself, since it would have to be active already before it was chosen. Thus the only remaining option is that ultimately certain facts have to be brute (such as the fact that this rather than that selector is in operation).

Parfit admits that one possibility is that there is no selector at all. This would mean that our actual world is chosen randomly, and that it has no particular features that would essentially differentiate it from all the other cosmic possibilities. In other words, our world would be a rather mediocre, unremarkable universe. And if there is no selector at the selector level, this most probably means that at the meta-level the operating selector is based on simplicity, since the situation in which there is no selector seems to be the simplest of all scenarios. It is interesting to observe that simplicity acting on the meta-level produces a world which is non-empty, whereas the same simplicity acting on the selector level clearly favors nothingness as the actual possibility.

Jim Holt uses the assumption that no meta-selector can pick out itself in his own proposal of how to solve the mystery of existence. More precisely, his argument is based on two general premises: the Principle of Sufficient Reason (for each truth there is an explanation of why it is true) and the Axiom of Foundation (no truth can explain itself). The task of explanation required by the first Principle begins with level 0 which contains all cosmic possibilities reality can take on. On level 1 we can find all possible explanations of the actual structure of the real world given in the form of various Selectors. And level 2 contains meta-Selectors, i.e. features that potentially explain which selector from level 1 is operating. On the basis of Foundation Holt eliminates all possible meta-Selectors except two: Fullness and Simplicity. That is, Holt argues that all the other selectors would select themselves, which is not allowed. For instance, Goodness, when introduced on level 2, will select itself at level 1, because it is presumably the ethically best selector of all. Similar arguments apply to Mathematical Elegance or Causal Orderliness as Selectors.[16]

Having reduced the number of possible meta-Selectors to only two, Holt goes on to show that both meta-Selectors lead to essentially the same type of world. Simplicity as the meta-Selector picks out no selector at level 1, which means that at level 0 the world is chosen at random, and therefore it lack any remarkable features which would set it apart from the remaining cosmic possibilities. On the other hand, when we apply Fullness in order to choose a selector at level 1, this criterion admits all selectors with no exception. This looks like an impossible situation when it comes to selecting a world at level 0, since various selectors are mutually exclusive (you can't for instance have a world which would be both the simplest and the fullest of all worlds). But if we agree to apply all the selectors only insofar as they can be reconciled with one another, the result will be a "compromise" world whose features will be mediocre. Thus on both choices the world selected at level 0 will look unremarkable and average, keeping an equal distance from all possible extremes. In Holt's words, the world comes out to be "generic". And it has to be stressed that the entire argument offers an explanation of such a world which does not leave any brute, unexplained facts, nor does it lead to a dangerous infinite regress.

11 THE SELF AND DEATH

If our world is indeed a run-of-the-mill, average universe with no special features which could account for its existence, then likewise the fact that it contains conscious beings such as ourselves should not count for much. In this perspective, the presence of humans has no higher purpose or deeper meaning. The coming into being of each individual human person is an amazing coincidence from a statistical point of view. The number of all available combinations of genes that give us our unique identity is the staggering 2^{30000}. Given that the estimated number of all people that have been born so far is 40 billion, it follows that the overwhelming majority of genetically possible humans have not come into existence. In a way we are lucky winners in an incredibly improbable cosmic lottery.

But there is an even deeper philosophical problem here. Improbable as it may be, does the selection of a given genetic combination ensure that a uniquely defined person will come into being? Each of us can ask the following question: could it happen that the person born with my genetic make-up was actually my identical twin, not me? We can go even further and ask: could I actually have been a different person, or an animal, or even a tree? A positive answer to such questions presupposes the existence of so-called Cartesian egos: individual mental substances which are only contingently associated with particular material structures such as brains. René Descartes (known also by his Latinized name Cartesius) famously argued for the existence of the unique subject of his thoughts (an "I") on the basis of his "Cogito, ergo sum" reasoning. He also added that this unique "I" (or "ego") is a purely mental entity, made up of thoughts only. But other philosophers were not entirely convinced by Descartes's argument. Some pointed out that we can only prove the existence of thoughts, and not of a thing that is thinking those thoughts. Hume for instance argued that there is no unique "self" independent of the mental states: thoughts, perceptions, memories, etc. Hume's conception of the mind is known as the bundle theory, because for him a person is no more than a loosely connected bundle of sensations, thoughts, and so on.

Modern philosophers tend to share at least some of Hume's skepticism regarding the existence of the inner "I". Parfit compares the self to a club which may change its members during its existence, and may temporarily cease to exist and later re-emerge in a different setting. Daniel Dennett reduces the inner "I" to a set of biological and social functions. Galen Strawson believes that at each moment a different self occupies our consciousness, so that there is no identity between various stages of our mental development. And for Thomas Nagel the true nature of our inner selves will forever be hidden from us.

Those who want to hold on to the notion of an inner "I" have to accept its two apparently contradictory characteristics. First of all, the self is the subject of consciousness – it is the thing that thinks, sees, and remembers. But at the same time the self seems to be also an object of consciousness, because we are clearly aware of being "ourselves". We identify and perceive our inner "self" as the subject of all thoughts. But how can an entity be the subject and the object of consciousness at the same time? Some philosophers, among them Ludwig Wittgenstein, deny that we can actually perceive our inner "I". As the eye cannot see itself, so we are incapable of perceiving our inner selves.

Philosophers have long debated the issue of personal identity. What makes a given person identical with him/herself and distinct from every other person in the world? One commonly accepted criterion of personal identity is the psychological criterion of self-identity. On this approach what defines a person is the totality of his/her thoughts, emotions, and memories. But the psychological criterion has problems with cases of amnesia, as well as hypothetical cases of "memory transplants". Another possible solution to the problem of self-identity is the physical criterion, which associates the identity of a person with the identity of his/her body. According to this approach it is in principle impossible to retain one's own self in a different material setting – whether in another body, or a computer. But another controversial consequence of this position stems from the fact that the physical identity of the brain is not an all-or-nothing affair. We can for instance perform a surgery on the brain of a patient removing some of its portions without disrupting its vital functions. As the resulting brain will not be identical with the brain before the surgery, the question arises whether the person after the surgery is identical with the person before. For Parfit this shows that ultimately the question of personal identity is meaningless. There is no fact of the matter about whether I now am the same person as I was ten years ago. In a sense, the Cartesian ego is an illusion.

But why is this illusion so persistent? One explanation may be that the I is self-creating, i.e. the very act of thinking about itself conjures up the thinking self. Robert Nozick suggested that the Cartesian "cogito" does not describe a preexisting state of affairs, but instead creates a new one which is true by declaration. The idea of the self-creating I puts us on a path to the transcendental philosophy of Kant, Hegel, Fichte and Schelling. For Fichte the statement "$I = I$" is the only example of a genuine logical law, since it does not presuppose anything. In contrast with that, the usual expression of the law of identity "$A = A$" must assume that A already exists, hence that something exists. But the existence of the I is guaranteed by its power of self-creation. For Fichte, all knowledge is ultimately self-knowledge. The world is a creation of the transcendental subject. Even those who don't share solipsist-like sentiments with Fichte nevertheless admit that the self stands in the center of the world. We should distinguish here "my world", as seen from the perspective of the self, and the objective world. The latter one is seen from a centerless point of view – a position called by Nagel "the view from nowhere".

Nagel is mystified by the fact that, from the objectivist, centerless point of view, his particular self is localized in a tiny fragment of the universe occupied by Thomas Nagel's body, and is an entity which might not have existed at all. The sentence "I am Thomas Nagel" seems to be fully explicable in terms of its external truth conditions: it is a sentence which is true only when uttered by none other than Thomas Nagel. But this analysis does not capture the meaning of a closely related statement which can be also uttered by Nagel himself: namely, that Thomas Nagel is *me*. Each of us has this powerful sensation of the uniqueness of his or her own personal viewpoint, or the Cartesian ego. It seems perfectly possible that your person from an empirical standpoint would exist, and yet it would not be you but someone else (for instance it would be your twin).

The amazement at the fact that the world contains something that is a unique "me" is matched by the difficulty of imagining one's own non-existence. If I can't think about the world without thinking that it is my world, then how can I imagine a world without me? It seems that the world in which I don't exist is a world which itself does not exist. Even though the view that the existence of the world depends on the existence of the perceiving subject is a solipsist illusion, it is a powerful one. Freud and Goethe claimed that it is impossible to truly conceive one's own death. Of course a failure of imagination is not a proof of non-existence, hence it does not follow that there is no death. But other philosophers disagree that one's death is impossible to imagine. For Hume this is no more difficult – and no more frightening – than thinking about the time before one was born. Socrates calmly explained to his friends before his execution that there is no reason to fear death, because it is either like a dreamless slumber, or a transition to a better world.

One reason why we fear death may be that it gives us the prospect of permanently losing everything that is good in life. The fact that we can't experience this loss does not mean that it is not bad for us. But what if there are only bad things in one's life? Isn't it better to end a life full of suffering? Some philosophers argue that death deprives us of something more than pleasures. It deprives us of things that we feel, perceive and think of. Miguel de Unamuno goes as far as to claim that it is better to suffer eternal torment in hell than not to exist at all. Nagel adds to that an observation that we tend to think of our existence as a universe of possibilities which can stand on its own and does not need to be grounded in any contingent reality. But the prospect of death undermines this optimistic belief and therefore causes anxiety. On the other hand, Parfit's conception of the insubstantial nature of the self leads in the direction of lessening our fear of death. For Parfit death merely breaks some psychological and physiological continuities. Buddhist-inspired Schopenhauer praises the values of the unconscious eternity in which there is no suffering. And for Hegel death relieves us from the feeling of alienation caused by the dangerous and unfriendly world.

12 HIGHLIGHTS

There are three basic schools of thought regarding the possibility of answering the question "Why is there something rather than nothing?" The optimists believe that an answer to this question can be found. The pessimists claim that the answer exists but we will never be able to find it. And the rejectionists deny that the question is even meaningful.

Two main arguments against the possibility of nothingness are proposed: the observer argument and the container argument. The first alleges that we can't imagine a totally empty universe without introducing a conscious observer. The second purports to prove that the elimination of all objects in the universe would leave something behind: an empty container, or space.

The subtraction argument attempts to show that an empty universe is conceptually possible. This argument is based on three main premises: finiteness, contingency, and independence.

The concept of nothingness is logically consistent, as there is a variant of logic called free logic whose rules remain valid in empty universes containing nothing at all.

In a world with no temporal bounds each event can in principle be causally explained by an earlier occurrence, but it is unclear whether such an infinite chain of causes can be taken to explain the existence of the entire universe. Some point out that this procedure is a case of the inadmissible *causa sui* type of explanation.

Causal explanations have to rely on the laws of nature, and therefore cannot explain the existence and particular form of these laws. This fact makes it extremely unlikely that a causal explanation of the entire universe could be found.

The God hypothesis is often accepted as a plausible explanation for the world's existence due to its apparent simplicity. However, it is doubtful whether God is indeed a simple being. Furthermore, God's existence calls for further explanation, which can be provided in the form of self-causation or logical necessity.

Modern physics seriously considers the hypothesis of the multiverse, according to which our universe is only one of a multitude of different universes which exist parallel to each other. One motivation for the multiverse hypothesis is provided by the many worlds interpretation of quantum mechanics. Another route to the notion of the multiverse leads through the theory of chaotic inflation, which alleges that the Big Bang type events are common occurrences.

The phenomenon of quantum tunneling may be the key to understanding how a universe can come out of nothing. According to one hypothesis, the state of total nothingness is inherently unstable due to the violation of Heisenberg's uncertainty principle, therefore it immediately gives rise to an energy-carrying vacuum which then rapidly expands thanks to the process of inflation.

A non-causal explanation of the world's existence can be based on mathematics. But this requires that the existence of abstract mathematical objects be independently justified. The recently offered Indispensability Argument for the reality of mathematical objects treats them as theoretical posits which figure in our best empirical theories. But this argument does not establish that mathematical objects are ontologically independent of the world of experience, and therefore they cannot provide the basis of an explanation of the empirical world.

The advances of modern science lead to the dematerialization of physical objects which no longer display the features of impenetrability and sturdiness traditionally associated with matter. Instead, the physical world is often interpreted as consisting of structures with no objects, or of pure information with no physical foundation.

Consciousness is an element of reality which according to many philosophers can be reduced neither to physical processes, nor to the flow of information. According to the radical philosophical hypothesis known as panpsychism, each material object in the universe is endowed with some type of consciousness.

Axiarchism is a position according to which the world exists because it is ethically good, and there is a metaphysical need for the existence of a good universe. This controversial view rests on three fundamental assumptions: that ethical values exist objectively and independently of our minds, that the goodness of the world is sufficient to bring it into existence, and that our megauniverse is indeed maximally good.

The task of explaining the existence of the universe can be presented in a framework which uses the notion of the Selector: an essential feature that only the actual world possesses. While the Selector chooses among all possible alternative worlds, including the null world, the meta-Selector picks out the Selector from all the possibilities.

If we assume the Principle of Sufficient Reason (each fact has to have an explanation) and the Foundation Principle (no truth can explain itself), then it may be argued that only two selectors are admissible: Simplicity and Fullness. Both selectors lead to the choice of an average, mediocre world.

There are several competing philosophical conceptions of the self (of our consciousness). The conception of the Cartesian ego assumes that the self is an independent entity only contingently associated with the body. On the other hand, the bundle theory states that the self is just a combination of perceptions and thoughts. Those who reject the concept of the ego argue that there is no rational reason to be afraid of death.

NOTES FROM CURIOUS READER

[1] For Leibniz the Principle of Sufficient Reason had a strong theological rationale. God as an infinitely wise and rational being would not let anything happen in the world without a reason. Admitting that there are facts without a rational explanation would be equivalent in Leibniz's view to doubting in God's omnipotence and omniscience.

[2] Apart from the final causes Aristotle distinguished a thing's material cause (the matter which the thing is made of), its formal cause (the form, or shape of the thing), and the efficient cause (the thing or process that produced a given object).

[3] It should be noted here that the majority of the linguistic "paradoxes" associated with the word "nothing" are a direct result of the grammatical structure of the English language which does not admit double negations. For instance in Spanish the

sentence "Nothing is better than steak" can be expressed as "There is not nothing better than steak" (*No hay nada mejor que el bistec*).

[4] The only controversial feature of Rundle's argument seems to be the assumption that the truth of a given sentence implies the existence of a fact corresponding to this sentence. But many philosophers see this assumption, known also as the truth-maker principle, as undeniable. If there were no facts described by true sentences, what would make those sentences true?

[5] The application of the conservation principle in this argument may be seen as problematic. Each step in the elimination procedure can be interpreted as taking us from one possible world to another, and no physical law is assumed to hold across possible worlds. Even though in each possible world its own total charge may be conserved, this does not imply the absurd consequence that all possible worlds have the same total charge.

[6] However, it has to be kept in mind that some rules of logic valid in non-empty domains are no longer accepted in free logic. For instance, the logical rule which enables one to derive "There is a red object" from "All objects are red" is invalid in an empty domain.

[7] Mathematically speaking it is possible to add to an infinite set of ordered objects with no beginning a new element which by stipulation precedes all objects in the set. For instance let's take the set of whole numbers (integers), and let's put a new number α "in front" of it. The new structure will look like this: α, ..., -2, -1, 0, 1, 2, ...

[8] It seems that Hume's two arguments in a sense contradict each other, since the first one alleges that an explanation for the existence of the world is impossible, whereas the second one concludes that such an explanation is available, after all.

[9] But is the goodness of God a necessary part of the simplest theory explaining the world's existence, or is it an extra assumption? If the latter is the case, then what reasons do we have for believing that the ultimate cause of the universe is good?

[10] It has to be stressed that the notion of a multiverse introduced in the inflationary theory is fundamentally different from the multiverse posited by the many-worlds interpretation of quantum mechanics. According to the Everettian interpretation different worlds separate from each other at various moments of measurements, so the entire multiverse has a tree-like structure with new universes constantly branching off. In the inflationary model, on the other hand, a given universe from the moment of its creation is forever

isolated from the remaining ones, and does not produce any future copies of itself.

[11] Tunneling is a process, predicted theoretically by quantum mechanics and confirmed experimentally, by which a quantum particle can pass through an energy barrier which is impossible to penetrate according to classical physics. If a classical particle of a given energy is surrounded by a wall of higher energy (a so-called potential well), this particle cannot break loose from the entrapment. However, quantum mechanics predicts that there is a non-zero probability that the particle will "disappear" and "re-emerge" on the other side of the barrier.

[12] It is slightly baffling that nowhere in the book devoted to the problem of explaining the existence of the world does the author mention the famous Deductive-Nomological model of scientific explanation formulated by Carl Hempel and Karl Popper. According to this philosophical theory, to explain a given occurrence means to find a law of nature and appropriate initial conditions such that the given occurrence can be logically derived from the law and the initial conditions. Perhaps one reason for ignoring this approach is that it is clearly incapable of producing an explanation for the existence of the entire universe, as the initial conditions are clearly part of the universe. However, the author mentions numerous other less

well-known conceptions which fail even more spectacularly.

[13] Gödel's Incompleteness Theorem states that no mathematical theory which is at least as complex as arithmetic can produce proofs for all true statements expressed in the language of this theory. In other words, there is no finite, executable procedure which could enable us to select all true statements of a given mathematical theory. Penrose uses this fact to argue that humans can beat computers when it comes to finding mathematical truths.

[14] A similar idea of the three worlds was proposed and developed earlier by the philosopher Karl Popper.

[15] Pauli's exclusion principle states that particles of a special kind known as fermions can never occupy exactly the same state simultaneously. Initially the principle was postulated for electrons in an atom in order to explain the known atomic structures, but later it was generalized for other situations. Today Pauli's principle is seen as a consequence of the fact that all fermions of the same type can occupy only so-called antisymmetric states.

[16] The weakest point of Holt's argument seems to be that it actually doesn't offer a general proof that all possible selectors except Simplicity and Fullness are self-explanatory. He merely cherry-picks a few

typical cases and argues that they would select themselves at level 1. But this falls short of a proper proof. Actually, it is not difficult at all to come up with an *ad hoc* selector different from the two which would definitely not pick out itself. For instance if we chose the "King Midas" selector "being made entirely of gold" at level 1, it would not select itself from level 2, since the selector itself is not made of gold.

Also available from Curious Reader:

Good Habits, Bad Habits. A Critical Discussion of Charles Duhigg's "The Power of Habit"

Sweet Dreams. A Concise Summary of David K. Randall's "Dreamland: An Adventure in the Strange Science of Sleep"

Why There is No God. The Essence of Richard Dawkins's "The God Delusion"

Made in the USA
Lexington, KY
07 January 2014